P9-CNE-800

CASTLES
of EUROPE

Schloss Lichtenstein:
Schwabian Alps. Germany

CASTLES
of EUROPE

MOLLY MOYNAHAN

TIGER BOOKS INTERNATIONAL
LONDON

This edition published in 1993 by
Tiger Books International PLC, London

Published by special arrangement with
William S. Konecky Associates, Inc.

ISBN: 1-85501-307-X

Printed in Hong Kong.

CONTENTS

INTRODUCTION

In the ninth and tenth centuries Charlemagne's empire shattered into a hundred pieces followed by wave after wave of Viking raid and invasion. Feudal warfare was dominated by heavy cavalry and castles. As central government crumbled and ceased to protect community against community, it fell to the strongest and the richest, the landowner of each district, to provide protection and a place where anarchy might be lessened. The castle was the military answer to cavalry and a visible symbol of the new social order. The knights were a military elite who constituted the secular ruling class of feudal Europe. The castle provided the appropriate setting for this aristocracy whose members were both lords and mounted warriors.

Castles evolved in western Europe as an integral part of the development of feudalism. They were the most important secular buildings in medieval [western] Europe. As an architectural expression of feudal lordship, the castle was a residential fortress, private as opposed to communal.

From the eleventh century through the Middle Ages, castles became stronger and more elaborate. The castle had always had a dual nature as both a home and a fortress. But with a desire for an increase in comfort, a certain dichotomy became obvious. There was a decline in the emphasis on fortification.

In the early Middle Ages, vast tracts of Europe were covered by forests which could only be crossed by a few established tracks. The main routes generally followed the river valleys which was why castles proliferated along such valleys as the Rhine and the lower Seine. The defense of the castle, and the need for a close watch to the approaches to it, dictated its location in a commanding position.

In looking at castles, it is crucial to recognize that they were part and parcel of medieval life. During the great pilgrimages, the Crusades, and the spread of Christianity, castles often served as centers of information. Royal castles were usually in the custody of the king while baronial castles were the center of the lord's honor. One went to the castle to pay rent, to render service, to plead a lawsuit or to attend court. Castles and churches, secular and spiritual power, jointly symbolized the authority and divine order of the medieval world.

Eilean Donan Castle: Scottish Highlands

Eilean Donan Castle: Highlands
Standing guard on a small, rocky
island at the junction of three
lochs, facing the Isle of Skye,
Eilean Donan resembles the
popular idea of a Scottish
medieval castle. But the building
itself dates entirely from the
twentieth century when it was
rebuilt between 1912 and 1932
by Colonel Jon Macrae, a direct
descendant of the last constable
of the castle. The original castle
was one of many built by
Alexander II to protect Scotland
from the Norse raiders. It was
held for centuries by the earl of
Seaforth and met its doom in
1719 because of loyalty to the
Jacobite cause. It was
garrisoned by Spanish troops
supporting the Old Pretender
and thus bombarded by an
English man-of-war to rubble.

In the century before the Norman Conquest (1066) the Normans developed in their homeland two different types of castle, one made of timber and the other of stone. Great rectangular stone keeps were introduced to the British Isles after 1066. Rectangular keeps were followed by polygonal and round versions.

After the breakdown of negotiations over the Magna Carta in 1215, England very nearly became part of France. The future Louis VIII, son of Philip Augustus, landed with a great army in 1216 and warfare was conducted largely by sieges of towns and castles.

The constant that runs through the development of the castle in Great Britain is the ingenuity with which men made the most of their opportunities. The possibilities of the particular site had the greatest influence on the architecture of each castle. The early arrangement of mound (motte)· and bailey provided the basic and most logical pattern by which a castle could be built rapidly in a flat area. Within Britain, England was the first country to be dotted with Norman castles. There we find the most ancient and venerable castles and several that are still in use: Windsor, Warwick and the Tower of London.

In considering the distribution of castles in England, we must recognize the inevitability of their concentration in the frontier regions, in the southeast towards the Continent, in the north towards Scotland and, above all, in the wide band of country that formed the marches of Wales. Yet it is indisputable that there is no English county without a castle and even inland counties have a large number of surviving castle sites. It is the dual nature of the castle as both a fortress and a residence that provides us with an explanation. If we regard them as purely military tools, we must view their locations as tactical rather than strategic. The Welsh castles were erected by individual lords to protect their own holdings. The pattern was a result of the Norman Conquest and the Norman Settlement. Castles were the chief means by which an alien military aristocracy established itself in England and Wales.

The thirty-five-year reign of Edward I (1272–1307) marked an unprecedented period of castle building in England and Wales, particularly in North Wales where Edward had his worst political trouble. All of the royal castles were designed by Master James of St. George, a military engineer from Savoy in France. The native Welsh princes had never fully accepted English rule and frequently organized in revolt against the crown. Edward proposed to settle the problem by building a network of powerful castles around North Wales.

When Edward I turned from Wales to attempt the conquest of Scotland, he found that the Scots had already recognized the importance of castles, probably as a result of the Scottish government's instability. While the kings of Scotland adopted feudalism, the Highland contained clans whose allegiance was sworn to their own chieftains. Motte-and-bailey castles were introduced as a way to extend feudal control. The union of parliaments of Scotland and England seemed to ensure the Scots' loyalty to the crown. Despite the Jacobite uprisings of 1715 and 1745, the Scottish castle underwent a gradual transformation over two centuries to become what amounted to a turreted Edwardian country house.

Haddon Hall: Derbyshire
This rambling castle is the Derbyshire seat of the Duke of Rutland. Parts of the structure, including terraced gardens, date from the Middle Ages. Haddon Hall is a mixture of battlemented walls, towers and chimneys, standing above the river Wye.

Warwick Castle: Warwickshire
A magnificent castle rising sheer
above the river Avon, seat of
the earls of Warwick since the
eleventh century. Founded by
William the Conqueror in 1068,
it owes its present grandeur to
the fourteenth century
Beauchamp earls and provides
us with a fine example of
fourteenth century fortification
complete with dungeons.

Alnwick: Northumberland
Alnwick was besieged by
William the Lion, King of
Scotland in 1172 and 1174. On
the second try, the castle was
recaptured. In the fourteenth
century, Alnwick was bought
from the Bishop of Durham by
Henry Percy who began a major
renovation. Percy rebuilt the
shell keep by enlarging it with
seven semicircular towers
added in a form called a
clustered donjon. From 1404 to
1405 Percy rebelled against
Henry IV and the castle was
taken. In the nineteenth century
Alnwick was restored to its
original medieval appearance by
the architect Anthony Salvin.

Hampton Court Palace: London
Begun in 1514 as Cardinal
Wolsey's country house,
Hampton Palace was obtained
by Henry VIII before Wolsey's
fall from power. Henry enlarged
it; Charles I lived there both as
king and prisoner; Charles II
repaired it; and William and
Mary rebuilt it according to
designs by Sir Christopher
Wren. Some of the finest Tudor
architecture in Great Britain
combine with Wren's eye for
beauty to make a magnificent
Tudor palace.

Bodiam: Sussex
Bodiam Castle stands near the river Rother, between Kent and Sussex. It was built by Sir Edward Dalyngrygge who was granted permission to fortify his house against a possible invasion from France. As soon as it was finished the English regained control of the Channel and Bodiam became redundant. Dalyngrygge built a symmetrical quadrangular stone castle surrounded by an artificial lake. Bodiam fell into ruins but the outer walls were restored by Lord Curzon early in this century.

Orford Castle: Suffolk
Built by Henry II (1154–1189) to strengthen his royal authority, it was begun in 1165 and completed in 1173. Located on the Suffolk coast, Orford was designed to control the British port. The surviving structure gives us a rare look at a polygonal keep, an unusual shape for this period.

Dover Castle: Kent
When William the Conqueror defeated Harold II at Hastings he headed towards Dover where the Anglo-Saxons had already raised a burh. William improved this fortification by erecting a motte-and-bailey. Dover Castle has the most massive tower in Britain, an almost 100-foot cube with walls from seventeen to twenty-one feet thick. In 1216 the castle was besieged by Louis, son of the French king but saved when Louis returned to France.

Windsor Castle: Berkshire
The largest in England, Windsor Castle is one of the principal residences of the queen and covers nearly thirteen acres. The first castle on the site was set up by William the Conqueror in about 1070. In 1170 the fortifications of earth and timber were replaced by stone buildings. Other major additions were made by Henry III, Edward III, Edward IV, Henry VIII and Charles II. The present appearance of the castle is mainly due to King George IV, who employed the architect Jeffrey Wyatville.

Mount Orgueil Castle: Channel Islands
Located on Jersey's east coast, Mount Orgueil dominates the tiny village and harbor of Gorey. Its site on a massive outcrop of rock made it impossible to take under siege. Many of its original medieval buildings are still intact.

Glamis Castle: Tayside
Glamis is the castle mentioned in *Macbeth* as the location for the murder of Duncan's grandfather, Malcolm II. While this is not historically accurate it is true that Lady Janet Douglas, the widow of the Earl of Glamis, was seized by James V, and burnt at the stake as a witch. The monarch took the castle and lived there for four years. A large L-plan tower house, the castle which stands today was renovated and restored by Patrick, Lord Glamis, in 1606.

Balmoral Castle: Aberdeen ▶
Built under the direction of Victoria's consort Albert by the architect William Smith, Balmoral has remained a royal residence to the present day. Outstanding architectural features include castellated gables and a 100-foot high tower.

Glamis Castle: Tayside

Glamis Castle: Tayside
Stairway leading down into the
dungeons

Here are two views of Castle Stalker, which is dramatically situated on an islet in Loch Linnhe. It was built by the Stewarts of Appin, who figure in Robert Louis Stevenson's *Kidnapped*. James Stewart was tried for a murder, which he did not commit by a Campbell judge and jury. He was found guilty and hanged not far from the castle walls.

Inveraray: Argyll
An early Gothic Revival castle
built in the mid-eighteenth
century by Roger Morris. In
1773, Dr. Johnson journeyed
through Scotland and visited the
castle. His comment: "What I
admire here, is the total
defiance of expense."

Beaumaris: Anglesey
Last of Edward I's great ring of castles, Beaumaris was surrendered to the parliamentarians in 1648 but escaped the usual destruction. It remains one of the best preserved concentric castles in Britain.

Dover Castle: Kent (overleaf)

Chepstow: Gwent
Begun in 1068, Chepstow was one of the first stone castles in Britain. Standing strategically on a natural limestone ridge, Chepstow was chosen by the Earl of Hereford as the site on which to erect the first great stone towers in Britain.

Dromoland Castle: Co. Clare
Dromoland Castle stands on an
estate that was once the home
of the Kings of Ireland. It dates
from 1570 but underwent
massive reconstruction in the
early nineteenth century under
the direction of Sir Edmund
O'Brien, the Baron of Inchiquin.

IRELAND

Irish society prized ties of blood, kinship and loyalty more than did the Norman lords, who prized the private residence and stronghold. There is a story told of an Irish chieftain refusing a castle offered to him by the Normans, saying he'd rather have a castle made of bones to one of stone.

The chieftain's fortresses were intended as places where the chief and his followers could enjoy a measure of protection from man and animal and as a place to enclose their livestock. The hill forts of the Iron Age began about 500 B.C. Here whole hilltops were enclosed within dry stone walls with protective ditches dug around it. Ring-forts followed the hill fort and they actually lasted into the seventeenth century, when the chieftains were banished and the Plantations from England and Scotland were established.

Although the arrival of the castle is usually attributed to the influence of the Anglo-Normans in 1170, records indicate the building of Irish castles as early as 1120. Tirlogh O'Conor, King of Connaught, was supposed to have erected a castle in 1129 in Athalone.

The Anglo-Normans brought the feudal system to Ireland. The king's vassals, the barons, commanded a corps of knights whose service to the sovereign was assured. In a hostile country such as Britain was when they came from Normandy, and as Ireland was when they came from England and Wales, there was a great need for a fortified residence that would serve as both a house and a defensive stronghold strategically situated for controlling the occupied land.

During the initial phase of the Anglo-Norman arrival in Ireland, a stone-built keep with a surrounding curtain wall was considered sufficient for defensive needs. Some castles further protected their entrance by constructing a barbican, which was a second building in front of the castle. Architecture was determined by military need and strategy. Flanking towers were added to protect vulnerable angles.

Cities were also fortified and Dublin was walled between 1204 and 1221. By the middle of the thirteenth century, major cities like Dublin and Limerick had castles but so did smaller Irish towns.

In 1429, Henry VI encouraged loyal English subjects to build castles by offering them a subsidy. At the end of the sixteenth century, the development of efficient heavy artillery meant the destruction of Irish castles hitherto considered impregnable. The armies of Elizabeth and Cromwell efficiently levelled many edifices. There was a brief revival in building between 1750 and 1775 when the taste for a style dubbed "Gothick" came to Ireland, meaning the use of Gothic trimming without altering the style of the building. Two leading English architects, Wyatt and Nash, designed both neoclassical and Gothick houses.

Dromoland Castle: Co. Clare
Located on acres of grounds, Dromoland Castle includes a folly built by Sir Edward O'Brien in the eighteenth century as a monument to his race horse.

City Walls: Dublin
Part of the old city walls that at one time ringed Dublin.

Bunratty Castle: Co. Clare
Bunratty is here pictured with flags flying from the battlements.

Bunratty Castle: Co. Clare
In 1277 Sir Thomas de Clare built a stone castle and a town grew up around its walls. Bunratty and the surrounding town were burnt down by the widow of the son of Sir Thomas. Bunratty passed back and forth between the Irish and the English until 1450 when Macon MacSioda Macnamara and his son Sean Finn erected the present castle.

Blarney Castle: Co. Cork
Blarney Castle was built in the fifteenth century as a stronghold for the McCarthys. It houses the famous Blarney Stone, which is supposed to endow the gift of eloquence on anyone who kisses it.

Birr Castle: Co. Offaly
Built about 180 feet from the medieval stronghold of the O'Carrols, in 1537 Birr was seized by the British and the submission of the chief was secured. Sir Lawrence Parsons, the attorney-general for Munster, renovated and enlarged the O'Carrol castle by rebuilding an important gate house with flanking, freestanding towers. In 1643 the castle was besieged by the Irish, who forced Sir Lawrence's son to surrender it. In 1650 the Parliamentarians took it back from Confederate Catholics, who set fire to it before leaving. In 1801, the second earl of Rosse embellished, refaced and gothicized the front of the existing house.

Knappogue: Co. Dublin
This castle was the home of the
MacNamara clan. Built in 1467 it
housed a succession of Norman
and Irish families until 1923
when it was partially destroyed
by fire. It has now been
beautifully restored as a fine
example of the diversity of
styles characteristic of the late
medieval period.

Kilkea Castle: Co. Kildare
This is reputed to be the oldest
inhabited castle in Ireland. It
dates from 1180. With its
imposing towers and walls it is
an unmistakable example of
Norman architecture.

Dungarvan: Co. Waterford
Anglo-Norman ruins dating from
1185. The keep and
battlemented walls are still
impressive, although the rest of
the structure stands in ruins.

Cliffs of Moher: Co. Clare
The impressive Cliffs of Moher
look out upon the Atlantic. They
were named after the Fort of
Mothar, which was destroyed
during the Napoleonic Wars.
Now only a signal tower stands
vigil on the lonely cliffs.

Ashford Castle: Co. Mayo
Ashford Castle is here seen
from two perspectives. It was
built by Sir Edward Guinness on
the banks of Lough Corrib, close
to the ruins of an old abbey at
Cong, in 1870. The architect
was Joseph Franklin Fuller who
designed the exterior to indicate
the impregnable facade of a
powerful medieval prince, while
the interior had all the amenities
of a late nineteenth century
country house. The castle
incorporates a medieval tower
house, bridge, water gate,
towers and turrets.

FRANCE

The origins of the French chateaux are the Roman castra, which were rebuilt and renamed as castel and then chateaux or chateaux forts. After Charlemagne's death came the Treaty of Verdun in 853, a tripartite division which recognized the Kingdom of the West Franks (France), the Kingdom of the East Franks (Germany) and the Middle Kingdom extending from the Low Countries to Italy. As the effective power of the kings declined, society became more and more based upon local territorial lordship.

Feudalism brought a sense of order to a country that had lost its centralized state. Chateaux were necessary in a land where seigneurs spent their time defending their holdings. As seats and symbols of feudal authority, chateaux served to provide shelter for the lords, their families and vassals.

The chateaux forts were built on a massive scale and were very difficult to enter. Their chief characteristic was the donjon or keep, which housed the seigneur and his family. By the mid-tenth century, castles were a familiar feature of the landscape, at least in northern France.

Throughout the Romanesque (1050–1150) and Gothic (1150–1500) periods, the church was very strong. All chateaux had chapels and the soaring architecture could be viewed as an expression of spiritual longing. Turrets were peaked and tall conical roofs topped even the weightiest towers.

Chateaudun: Normandy
This castle stands on a promontory that reaches into the Loire Valley. It probably dates from the twelfth century despite the inscription, over the entrance to its impressive cylindrical keep, that bears the name Thibaut le Tricheur, a tenth century count of Blois.

Carcassonne: (overleaf)
Provence
Located in the fortified medieval
town of the same name, the
castle was built in the twelfth
century.

The religious conflict between the Huguenots and the Catholic League influenced the chateaux architecture in the sixteenth century. Chateaux were made more luxurious—Renaissance obsessions with balance and perspective, light and symmetry, were applied. Windows were added to stout outer walls, classical ornamentation —columns and pilasters, dormers with pediments like temple fronts—were added. Gardens were designed to reflect this longing for order and beauty. Flowers were geometrically arranged, and clipped hedges lined carefully arranged paths.

In 1598 the Edict of Nantes settled the religious crisis, and in the seventeenth century France held a dominant position in culture and politics. Louis XIV was determined to uproot the aristocrats from their lands and bring them under his own personal control in court. During the period of the Revolution and the Empire (1789–1815), very few new chateaux were built and a considerable number were destroyed. After the Restoration, building resumed and reached unprecedented levels during the Second Empire and the Third Republic.

Angers: Loire Valley
Angers is one of the most imposing castles in France. Built in the form of an irregular pentagon, it boasts seventeen drum-towers. It was destroyed by Henri III and not restored until the 1950s. Today it houses a tapestry museum that includes the famous Apocalypse series of Nicholas Bataille.

Anjony: Auvergne
Built between 1435 and 1440,
Anjony reflects a rare unity of
architectural style, late feudal
Gothic. The Anjony family had
the patronage of the French
king but was mired in a blood
feud with another clan, the
Tournemires, who supported
England against France in the
Hundred Years War. Bernard
D'Anjony married Marguerite de
Tournemires but he built his
fortress on land originally
claimed by the Tournemires and
for the next two centuries these
families were at war.

Chaumont: Loire Valley
Chaumont overlooks the Loire.
It was erected by Pierre
d'Amboise in the late fifteenth
century and later was the home
of Catherine de Medici, widow
of Henri II. She installed her
astrologer in a room connected
by a staircase to the top of the
tower, which he used as an
observatory. In 1809 Napoleon
banished Mme. de Staël to
Chaumont.

Pierrefonds: Valois
Towered, turreted, gabled and
dormered, Pierrefonds is a
monumental reconsturction of
an authentic fourteenth century
chateau fort. Reconstructed by
engineer/architect Viollet-le-Duc
in 1857, the castle was originally
built during the last decade of
the fourteenth century by
Charles V's second son Louis,
duc d'Orleans. Pierrefonds
represents Second Empire
taste, as much as its medieval
origins, with picturesque detail
and deliberate asymmetry.

Chaumont: Loire Valley
The grim-looking fortress
contains many treasures:
tapestries, fine furnishings and a
collection of glass and
medallions engraved by the
eighteenth century Italian
artist, Nini.

Chateau Palmer:
Cantenac-Margaux
The name Chateau Palmer is
most closely identified with
wine. The Chateau itself is a
small but lovely example of 19th
century French architecture. It
bears the name of Major
General Charles Palmer, the first
proprietor of the vineyard.

Chateau Vitré: Brittany
Vitré is the best preserved
ancient town in Brittany. The
castle, first constructed in the
eleventh century, was rebuilt
300 years later during the
golden period of Breton military
architecture. It overlooks the
Vilaine Valley.

Sully: Loire Valley (overleaf)
This elegant chateau, a mixture of styles from various periods, is built right on the banks of the Loire. The northern part of the chateau, facing the river, dates from the fourteenth century. It was here that Georges de la Tremouille received Joan of Arc.

Chateau du Taureau: Brittany
This medieval fortress was built on an islet by Francois I to guard the port of Morlaix.

Chateaudun: Normandy

Aigues-Mortes: Provence
Built in 1240 by Saint Louis to
establish the kingdom of
France's first Mediterranean
seaport. Saint Louis embarked
on the Seventh Crusade from
Aigues-Mortes and then to
Tunis in 1270 where he died.
The castle was completed by
Philip the Bold, who finished the
massive ramparts, thirty feet
high and twenty feet thick,
containing twenty towers and
ten gates. During the Hundred
Years War, Burgundians
captured the town but were
then massacred while sleeping,
and their mutilated bodies
thrown into what is now known
as The Tower of the
Burgundians.

L'Archambault: Yonnè
Ruined fortress in the lovely
countryside of the Yonne region.

La Brede: Bordeaux
First fortified in the eleventh
century by the lords of La
Lande, here is where
Charlemagne is supposed to
have slept following the Battle
of Roncevalles. La Brede was
the home of the political
philosopher Montesquieu
(1680–1755). La Brede has
changed little since its
reconstruction in 1419, as a
small but heavily fortified
polygonal complex at the edge
of the forests of La Lande,
south of Bordeaux. Dominating
the complex of turrets,
buttresses, peaked summits,
half-timbered upper stories and
flat, red-tiled roofs is the tall
donjon crowned by an enclosed
lookout passage for sentinels.

Kasteel De Haar: Haarzuylens De Haar was built in the thirteenth century but was destroyed in 1482. The rebuilt castle is located in a low area near the Rhine but the first castle was probably built on a higher piece of ground, or haar, from which it took its name. The reconstructed castle is the largest in the Netherlands. P. J. H. Cuypers, a well-known Dutch architect, was commissioned in 1892 to totally renovate the second De Haar. Cuypers used old drawings and prints of the medieval facade but created an entirely original entrance. The interior of De Haar is entirely Neo-Gothic.

Following the disintegration of the Carolingian Empire, the Low Countries suffered both war and invasion. Founded by such men as Dirk I (Theodoric of Holland) and Godfrey I, strong local feudal dynasties emerged that built castles within their domains. Castle building in the Netherlands was scarce until brickmaking developed enough to compensate for the lack of other natural building materials. Until the nineteenth century, when the Amsterdam-Rhine canal was opened, the most direct water link between Utrecht and the ports of the North Sea was the river Vecht. Waterways in Holland represented the country's lifeblood. Most Dutch medieval castles were built along the Langbroekerwetering due to the Bishop of Utrecht and the dean of his cathedral awarding parcels of this land to individuals who had performed valuable service.

Landowners normally built their keeps here. Although these houses were often rebuilt and renovated, the keeps remained. Examples of stone ring-walls also survive from the twelfth century. The somewhat monotonous architecture of Dutch castles, being of the lowland, moated type, is most likely influenced by the country's flat terrain.

In the thirteenth century, Floris IV, Count of Holland, gave great impetus to the building of castles with Muiderslot, which shows strong French influence in its drum towers and rectangular layout. A characteristic of the medieval fortress residence is this square plan where the living quarters surround an inner court. Muiderslot was an exception to the simplicity of most Dutch castles. In the sixteenth century Renaissance style influenced the rebuilding with shell-and-mask motifs, gables and pilasters added on. Many of these square castles appeared after 1250, and it is believed that they were introduced by the Crusaders returning from the Holy Land.

In the seventeenth century excessive decoration fell out of fashion. The Dutch style was one of unity between house, garden and interior. The domestic concerns of the Establishment took precedence over great displays of wealth or armor. In the end, many Dutch castles were simply converted into residences.

Castle Stapelen: Boxtel
The first mention of Castle Stapelen was in 1293, as residence of the Barons of Bostel. The building was extensively renovated during the second half of the nineteenth century, resulting in a jumble of battlements, towers and stepped gables.

Castle Haamstede: Haamstede
While the tower of Castle Haamstede dates from the thirteenth century, the building was enlarged and rebuilt after a fire in 1525 and again renovated in 1609, with a bridge and a small gate added.

Muiderslot: Muiden
The current Muiderslot was built on the foundation of the razed castle, from 1370 to 1386. Robert Dudley, earl of Leicester, lived there during his time as governor of the Netherlands, and Pieter Corneliszoon Hooft, a poet, playwright and historian, created an artistic renaissance based in the castle from 1613 to 1647. The facade of Muiderslot is forbidding, but the castle shows strong French influence in its drum towers and rectangular layout. A covered walkway runs the length of the curtain wall.

Castle Stapelen: Boxtel

Castle Beverweerd: Werkhoven
Rebuilt in Neo-Gothic style between 1835 and 1840 from the ruins of a thirteenth century tower or keep, Castle Beverweerd is located on the river de Kromme Rijn. From 1600 to 1665 the Lord of Beverweert was Lodewijk van Nassau-Odijk, son of the Prince of Maurits.

Castle Sandenburg: Langbroek
Originally a fourteenth century manor house, Sandenburg was enlarged with a large square tower and a pointed roof in the eighteenth century. Battlemented turrets were also added later. The castle is situated on the Langbroekse Wetering River in a large tree-filled park.

Muiderslot: Muiden

Loewenburg:
Kassel-Wilhelmshohe
Duke Wilhelm IX in 1793
ordered his architect Heinrich
Christoph Jussow to build him a
residence in the form of a
medieval ruined castle. Today it
houses a museum. In the
background one can see the
Herkules, an elaborate Baroque
construction completed a
century earlier.

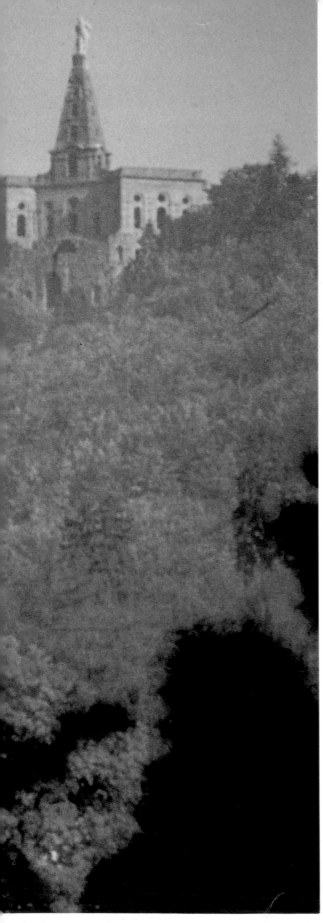

GERMANY & AUSTRIA

Early medieval defenses in Germany were generally of earth and timber, motte-and-bailey-type castles being common in low-lying areas. In mountainous country they were more likely to consist of simple stone enclosures. From the eleventh or twelfth century, tall towers were a common feature of such castles. The Hohenstafen emperors (1152–1250) engaged in systematic fortress building to consolidate their rule. The distinction between palace and castle in Germany was a legal one: the palace had imperial, administrative status and was probably situated in or near a town. However, its physical layout was identical to that of a castle. The castle generally consisted of a tall tower, a curtain wall with a palace, residential buildings and a chapel. In addition, it had three main functions: first, as a fortified seat of a lord; second, as a legal center; and third, as a status symbol.

In 1152, King Frederick I, Barbarossa, was chosen as emperor by the princes of Germany. Barbarossa, a member of the new nobility that had arisen at the expense of imperial lords, was committed to the new feudal society. Coming from a family known for its castle building, he was thought to have built 350 palaces and castles that were under the command of Ministerriales. Barbarossa considered himself the heir not only of Charlemagne but of the entire ancient Roman Empire. He had a taste for grand effects; fortifications were added as an afterthought.

As trade increased, richer burghers built themselves houses of stone, and bishops and dukes built castles. One of the chief reasons for the individual nature of German castles was geographical. Many of the best castle sites

were located on mountains above frequented routes like the Rhine. The castles extracted a heavy toll from the traders who depended on access to major rivers to move their goods. In the thirteenth century, leagues were formed by cities to fight the occupants of the castles.

The political fragmentation and weakening of the imperial power which followed the collapse of the Hohenstaufen dynasty created conditions favorable to castle building. Late in the twelfth century, the Teutonic order was founded in the Holy Land. By 1283 the knights were masters of the country and in the fourteenth century they produced the most sophisticated and original forms of German castles. Castles in Austria followed a similar pattern to those in Germany. The mountains of Austria produced many hilltop strongholds and, like in Germany, there was a tendency to reinforce already existing fortresses built on impregnable sites. Probably between 1253 and 1278, during the reign of the king of Bohemia and duke of Austria, a number of moated castles with regular rectangular plans were built in lower Austria.

Burg Rheinstein:
Trechtingshausen
Originally dating from the
Middle Ages, the castle fell to
ruins in the sixteenth century. In
1823 it was rebuilt in
Neo-Gothic style as a summer
house by a Russian prince.

Reichsburg: Cochem
This stunning fortress with its
vantage of the Mosel River was
once an imperial residence.
Construction was begun on it in
1027. The castle comes
complete with a secret
passageway that winds eerily
into its depths.

Goetzenburg Castle: Jagsthausen

The birthplace of Goetz von Berlichingen, the Knight of The Iron Fist. Goetz was immortalized by the playwright Goethe, who wrote his play *Goetz von Berlichingen,* detailing the exploits of this warrior knight. Goetzenburg has remained the seat of the Berlichingen family. While the castle has been renovated many times, the north wing remains virtually unchanged. The castle has a museum where the iron hand is available for viewing.

Burg Hohenstein: Taunus
Built in 1190 by Duke von Katzenelnbogen in the forest of Taunus, Hohenstein was enlarged in 1422 by Johann III and renovated again in 1604. The castle was destroyed during the Thirty Years War.

Burg Hohenstein: Taunus
Section of ramparts.

Schloss Langenberg:
Langenberg
This Renaissance palace with its
lovely arcaded inner courtyard
was built in 1610 by the prince
of Hohenlohe.

Burg Eltz: Moselkern
Built between the twelfth and
sixteenth centuries, Burg Eltz is
like a fairy-tale castle, with its
spires, towers, graceful lines
and mysterious forest setting. It
is located on the Elzbach River.

Schloss Braunfels: Braunfels
The original castle of the counts
of Solms dates back to 1250.
After many remodellings the
castle acquired its present form
in 1885. It is an excellent
representative of the archaizing
tendencies of the late
nineteenth century.

Schloss auf der Pfaueninsel: Berlin
This castle, built in 1794 by Friedrich Wilhelm II, king of Prussia, was designed to suggest a ruined fortress. It sits on Peacock Island in the Wannsee section of Berlin.

Strahlenburg: Schriesheim ▶
The ancient castle Strahlenburg was built by Conrad I von Hirschburg in the middle of the twelfth century. A seventy-foot tower and one wall are all that remain of the original castle. Later it was rebuilt by Hartmut von Croneberg. It now stands partially in ruins.

Schloss Braunfels: Braunfels
Schloss Braunfels houses a
wonderful collection of art that
is open to the public.

◀ Wartburg Castle: Eisenach
Established in 1067 by Ludwig
the Leaper, the first of the
House of Ludowinger. In 1130
the Holy Roman Emperor
Lothair raised the House of
Ludowinger to the position of
Princes. During the reign of
Ludwig III (1172–1190) the
family acquired a great deal of
land.

Burg Tierberg: Braunsbach
Situated in a commanding
hillside position, Tierberg was
constructed under the direction
of the Hohenlohe family from
whom this region of Germany
takes its name.

Die Schoenberg: Oberwesel
The Schoenberg is located on a
high hill overlooking the Rhine.
Built in the thirteenth century as
a spacious fortress, it was
destroyed in 1689. The castle is
now a picturesque ruin.

Marksburg: Braubach
The Marksburg is one of Germany's most beautiful castles. Situated on cliffs overlooking the Rhine, it is the only castle in the region that was never destroyed. Built in 1100, remodelled during the thirteenth and fourteenth centuries, it provides us with a vivid picture of the life and customs of the feudal age. Today it houses the Deutsche Burgenvereinigung, a society dedicated to the preservation of German castles.

Schloss Lichtenstein:
Schwabian Alps
Perched on a rock high above
the valley floor, a product of the
romantic passion for castles in
the nineteenth century. It was
built from 1840 to 1841 by Duke
Wilhelm of Urach.

Schloss Lichtenstein:
Schwabian Alps
The castle has preserved a fine
collection of medieval armor.

Vaduz Castle: Duchy of
Liechtenstein
A hilltop fortress dating to
Roman times, Vaduz Castle was
built in the thirteenth century but
fell into ruins and has been rebuilt
several times. It is now the
residence of Franz Joseph II.

Wasserburg Gemen: Borken
A fine example of an eighteenth
century water castle.

Schloss Mespelbrunn:
Mespelbrunn
This small castle is located in
the Spessart Woods. Originally
built in 1430, it was enlarged to
its present size a century later.

Burg Hohenzollern: Hechingen
Built in the eleventh century,
Hohenzollern has been
destroyed and rebuilt several
times. King Friederich Wilhelm IV
of Prussia had it rebuilt in its
present romantic form. The
chapel contains the tombs of
King Friederich-Wilhelm I and
Frederick the Great.

Hohenzollern Crown
The Hohenzollerns were the
rulers of Prussia. Their crown
jewels are kept at Burg
Hohenzollern, their ancestral
seat.

Burg Hohenzollern, Hechingen

Burg Linn: Krefeld
Burg Linn is a water castle that
dates from the medieval period.
At the end of the Middle Ages a
wall ringing the castle was
erected. This picture presents a
view of the castle through the
only remaining portal in the ring
wall.

Schloss Marienberg: Pattensen
Begun in 1858, Marienberg is a
fine example of Neo-Gothic
architecture. It was built for the
wife of George V, the last king
of Hanover.

Burg Schleinitz: Eggenburg
The orignial castle was built in
the thirteenth century, but its
present form dates back to the
late seventeenth century.

Burg Mautendorf: Mautendorf
Castle Mautendorf was
sponsored by Pope Innocent IV
who decreed in 1253 that
Mautendorf, a market town,
should have a castle. Ownership
of the castle went to the Turks
in 1482 but in 1490 reverted to
Salzburg. In the fifteenth and
sixteenth centuries, Mautendorf
was enlarged with the addition
of a small tower and the entire
building was restored and rebuilt
in the nineteenth century.

Burg Rastenberg: Zwettl
Dating from 1188, in 1205 Rastenberg was owned by Hugo von Rauhenegger. Wilhalm von Neideckh zu Rastenberg built a reinforced castle around the existing building. In 1620, during the Thirty Years War, the castle was half destroyed. In the eighteenth century the castle was reconstructed with most of its Renaissance architecture changed to baroque. In 1790 the castle was again destroyed. The count of Thurn-Valsassina whose family has owned Rastenberg since 1872 rebuilt the castle which still stands today.

Wasserschloss Anif: South of Salzburg
A characteristic water castle built on a lake, Anif was built in the sixteenth century by the Archbishop of Salzburg. In 1803, Count Arco-Stepperg bought the castle and, between 1838 and 1848, enlarged it. The abdication of King Ludwig III von Bayern occurred here in 1918. The castle contains an outstanding collection of Romanesque furniture.

Burg Rappottenstein:
The great Watch Tower of
Rappottenstein Castle dates
from the twelfth century, with
other parts of the castle being
added on during the following
200 years. The castle has been
in the family of Abensberg-
Traun for more than 300 years.

Burg Liechtenstein: Modlingen
One of the oldest Austrian
castles, Liechtenstein dates
from 1100 and was originally
built of wood. A follower of the
aristocracy of Schwarzenburg
who called himself von
Liechtenstein added a stone
tower and a chapel. In the
thirteenth century his
descendants constructed a new
castle with two towers. In 1529
the castle was destroyed by the
Turks and it was abandoned
until 1808, when Prince Johann I
von und zu Liechtenstein bought
the ruins. He then hired the
architects Gangolf Kayser and
Humbert Walcher von Moltheim
to renovate it as a Romanesque
castle.

Schloss Schonbuhel:
Rebuilt in 1821 on the ruins of a
twelfth century fortress, the
castle perches on the rocky
right bank of the Danube.

Salzburg Castle: Salzburg
Built in 1077 on a cliff
overlooking Salzburg City, the
original building was constructed
of wood. Salzburg is the largest
castle in Austria.

Neuschwanstein Castle: Schwangau
Construction was begun by King Ludwig II, the mad king of Bavaria, in 1870. This archetype of the German fairy-tale castle is surrounded by snow covered peaks and deep woods. Ludwig was obsessed with this castle, but he did not live to see it completed. Here the castle is seen from two vantages.

Before the late Middle Ages, Swedish nobles lived in simple surroundings, usually in a timbered two-room house. These dwellings were distinguished from farmhouses by their grander size and often the addition of some sort of fortress feature like a stone wall or tower.

During the twelfth century, defense and dwelling were to be united, and features such as moats and ramparts became more common. King Gustav Vasa was one of the first to build a castle. During his reign (1521–1560), the monarchy gained the upper hand in the parliament, which consisted of the four estates: nobility, clergy, burghers and landowning farmers. Kingship became hereditary and during this time of Reformation, the king made himself the head of the Swedish Church, centralizing the administration of the government, following Germany's example.

The Renaissance came to Sweden with King Gustav's sons. Stockholm's palace was rebuilt with the help of imported architects and engineers. The proliferation of pirates along the east coast of Sweden inspired the building of a series of castles whose architecture clearly showed both French and German influences. During the late Middle Ages, the rising nobility built Sweden's monumental houses. After the Peace of Westphalia in 1648, construction reached its peak but the reign of Karl XII (1697–1718) brought more war and it was a long time before the ruined land was rebuilt.

In Denmark the first stone castles were built during the 12th century. The building of castles was done by the bishops, who were extraordinarily rich and powerful. Archbishop Eskil constructed a stone castle at Syborg in 1150 on a site previously occupied by an octagonal wooden tower. In 1211 Archbishop Abaslom built the fortress, which formed the center of Copenhagen. As the Danish monarchy grew stronger in the early thirteenth century, so did the number of castles under royal control.

Egeskov Castle: Funen Island Built in 1554 by Frands Brockenhuus, Egeskov is located in the middle of a small lake. The fortress includes embrasures and machicolations and a drawbridge. It is said the castle was named Egeskov (oak forest) because a whole oak forest was used for the foundation of the building.

DENMARK

Egeskov Castle: Funen Island

Kroneborg: Elsinore
This is the castle upon whose battlements Hamlet, Prince of the Danes, saw his father's ghost "doomed for a time to walk the night." Destroyed by fire in 1629 it was rebuilt by Christian IV. The chapel, which survived the fire, and the 200-foot-long Knight's Hall are two of its more interesting features.

Hammershus, Bornholm Island
This ruined castle stands on an
island east of Copenhagen; it
was built to protect the city
from possible attacks from
Sweden and Germany.

Kalmar Castle: Kalmar
Built on the site of a 1397
medieval castellum, Kalmar
Castle was rebuilt by Gustav
Vasa into a fortified Renaissance
palace. Kalmar fell to the Danes
in 1611 but was retaken and
restored. Vasa wanted a castle
capable of resisting attack from
either land or sea. In 1568, the
gateway into the outer courtyard
was reset so no one could fire
directly upon the castle's
defenders.

Gripsholm Castle:
Sodermanland
Gripsholm is located 48
kilometers southwest of
Stolkholm, on the shore of Lake
Malar. The castle was built in
the sixteenth century by
Gustavus Vasa on the site of a
fourteenth century structure.

Kalmar Castle: Kalmar

SPAIN

Spanish castles exist as part of their surroundings. They are an organic element of the landscape, unique to an architecture that usually overpowers its environment. While it is clear that this architectural integrity is a direct result of the military function of most Spanish castles, we are still amazed and impressed by the harmonious relationship between nature and structure.

The Spanish castle has its beginning in the castellum built by the Romans to defend Spain from the barbarians. The castellum was a fortress located in a strategic place to guard military encampments, coasts, roads or settlements. The center of the Iberian Peninsula is called Castilla or Castile: The Land of the Castles, and the importance of these structures cannot be exaggerated. During the Christian advance into Moorish territory, a campaign called the "Reconquest," recently conquered areas were repopulated in the shelter of the castles which also served as the chief residences of the local lords.

This process of reconquest, often viewed as a single wave of advance, was, in fact, punctuated by a series of advances and retreats and marked by fighting between the Christians themselves. This perpetual turbulence is one reason Spain is dotted with castles of all descriptions!

The most important element in the typical Spanish military castle was the tower of the lord, or the keep. If the castle fell into the hands of the enemy, the keep could still be defended. In front of this tower was a walled enclosure, either rectangular or square, called the bailey. In Moorish-influenced structures, there was also an *albacar*, a huge space connected with the castle, surrounded by a wall, where the village population would

Parador de Alcaniz: Teruel
The headquarters of the Order of Calatrava in the twelfth century, Alcaniz is now a monastery which contains in its Tower of Tribute preserved Gothic mural paintings. The castle is located on top of a hill which marks the center of town.

find refuge with their livestock during an attack. Along the walls were light constructions used for stables and stores. At the corners of the rectangle other towers were built to make defense easier. The fortress was entered by a draw-bridge since the castle was usually surrounded by a moat.

This design was a general plan for the Christian military castle but was frequently modified to accommodate the terrain. We can examine these modifications in two categories of Spanish castles: the rock castles and the mountain castles.

Rock castles were built on the steepest part of the rock. Until the invention of artillery, they were virtually impregnable. Because of their limited size, they had little offensive power and, with the development of a type of warfare that required greater mobility, the mountain castle became preferable. This type of castle had the form of a great ship with many walls and round towers surrounded by a moat.

As Christian control widened and an artistic sensibility flourished, the Gothic style became more common and Spanish castles began to look less militaristic. When the Catholic monarchs conquered the last Muslim refuge in the peninsula in 1492, they decreed that all old castles and fortified rocks should be demolished. From this time on, the warlike castle became history, and many castles were converted into luxurious residences. Of the 10,000 castles estimated to exist in the Middle Ages, there remain about 2,500. All of them have survived with their original character intact. Customs, wars, and the climate have neither hidden nor distorted these magnificent structures.

Parador Ciudad Rodrigo: Salamanca
A crenellated castle which sits on the banks of the Agueda River, it was built between 1334 and 1379 by Lope Arias for King Henry II of Trastamara. A Roman aqueduct and bridge mark the route called the Via de la Plata: The Silver Way.

Parador de Zamora: Zamora
A Renaissance palace built in 1459 by the first duke of Alba over the ruins of a Roman fort located in the center of the city of Zamora. The palace has an interior courtyard, typical of civil architecture in the Castile region.

Parador Ubeda: Jaén
Dating from the sixteenth
century, this palace was
renovated entirely in the
seventeenth. It belonged to Don
Fernando Ortega Salido, Dean of
Malaga and the first Chaplain of
the Sacred Chapel of the Savior.
He was best known as Dean
Ortega. Ubeda is a fine example
of Renaissance Andalusian
architecture.

Jarandilla de la Vera: Caceras
Construction on this castle,
begun in the late fourteenth
century, was completed in the
first years of the fifteenth. Built
for the Count of Oropesa, it
later became the home of
Emperor Charles V.

Parador de Siguenza:
Guadalajara
A Visigoth castle which was
rebuilt by the Arabs. In 1112 it
was reconquered and made into
an episcopal fortress by the
Christians. The throne hall and a
Romanesque chapel have been
preserved.

Parador de León: León
Built around 1515, the building
housed the Order of the Knights
of Santiago. Streams of pilgrims
on their way to Santiago da
Compostela would pray in the
chapel pictured here.

Parador de Oropesa: Toledo
This castle dates from the
Muslim period and was
reconstructed in the fifteenth
century. It was once the home
of the counts of Oropesa.

Parador de Zafra: Badajoz Zafra was built between 1437 and 1443. Hernán Cortés lived here before going off to the just discovered New World. The castle is a showcase for the artistic wealth of the period. The interior patio is built with Doric columns and is attributed to Juan de Herrera, the architect who designed El Escorial for Philip II. There is also a fine chapel.

Parador de Granada: Granada An Arab palace dating from the Nasrite dynasty (1302), it was built by Muhammad III and then restored by Yusef I (1334–1354) and again by Muhammad V (1354–1359). In the fifteenth century the Catholic monarchs, Isabela and Ferdinand, converted the palace into a Franciscan monastery situated on the grounds of the Alhambra. The palace has views of the Generalife Gardens, the Albaicin and the Sierra Nevada range.

Parador de Alarcon: Cuenca
A magnificent fortified castle
with battlements dating from
the eighth century, this Arab
monument is situated
dramatically on a hill,
surrounded by the Jucar River.

Parador de Tortosa: (overleaf)
Tarragona
The castle of "La Zuda," a
name which refers to a well,
was built by the Moorish King
Abderraman the First.

INDEX

CREDITS

Grateful acknowledgement is made to the following sources.

The Austrian Tourist Board pages 2, 86, 87, 94, 95, 96, 97, 98, 100, 101

The British Tourist Authority pages 11, 12, 13, 14, 15, 16, 18, 20, 21, 22, 23, 24, 25, 26, 28, 29

Burg Hotel Hohenstein page 78

Castle Reichsburg page 76, 77

The Danish Tourist Board—pages 104, 106, 108, 109

The Family Hermann Hecher page 75

The French Government Tourist Office pages 46, 49, 50, 52, 53, 54, 58, 59, 60, 62, 63, 64

The German Information Center pages 72, 79, 80, 82, 83, 84, 89, 90, 91, 92, 93, 102, 103

The Susan Griggs Agency page 88

The Irish Tourist Board pages 35, 36, 37, 38, 40, 41, 42, 44, 45

Kunstverlag F.G. Zeitz page 85

The National Tourist Office of Spain pages 112, 114, 116, 118, 119, 120, 121, 122, 124

The Netherlands Tourist Board page 66, 68, 69, 70

James Robinson pages, 6, 8, 17, 27, 56

The Swedish Tourist Board page 110

Adrian Taylor pages 32, 34, 35

Book designed by Adrian Taylor